To August
from Aunt Peach
Sunriver 2019

501
THINGS TO FIND

igloobooks

INTRODUCTION

Welcome to the exciting world of Joey JCB and all his JCB friends.
Follow the team around lots of fun JCB scenes and see if you can
find the hidden characters in each. Once you've found them,
see if you can find all the other hidden items as well.

Joey JCB

Larry Loadall

Elvis Excavator

Rex Roller

Max

Doug Dumptruck

Tommy Truck

Dan Dozer

Marty Mixer

Freddie Fastrac

Roxy Robot

Practice your JCB spotting skills and see if you can
find all 11 JCB friends on the opposite page?

PRACTICE SITE

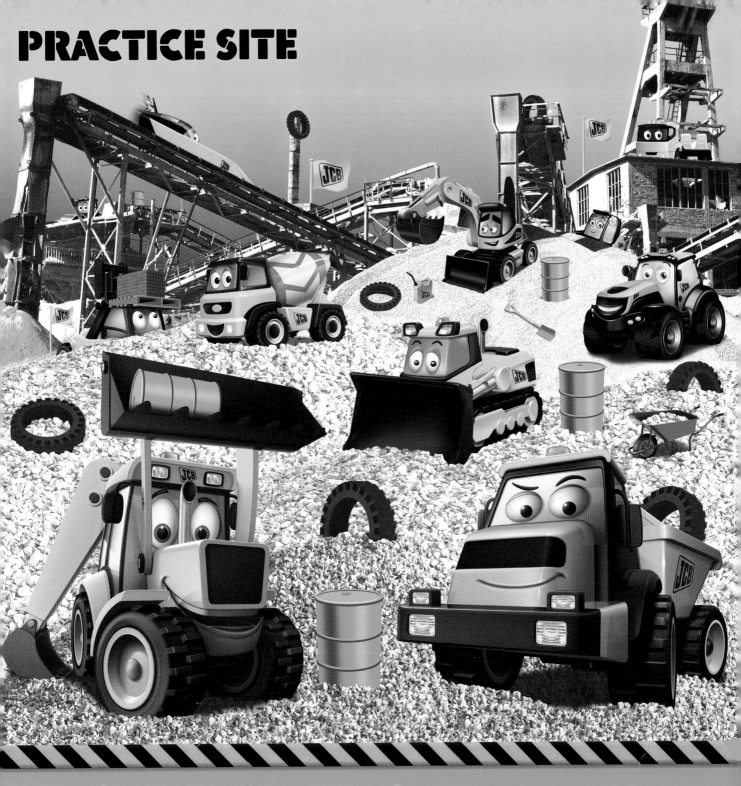

HIGHWAY MAYHEM

The JCB team are preparing a new super highway.
It's a very big task! Can you find Marty Mixer
and Rex Roller on the busy site?

Can you spot these things too?

1 crane

3 cement mixers

4 piles of rubble

6 toolboxes

8 spades

15 gold nuggets

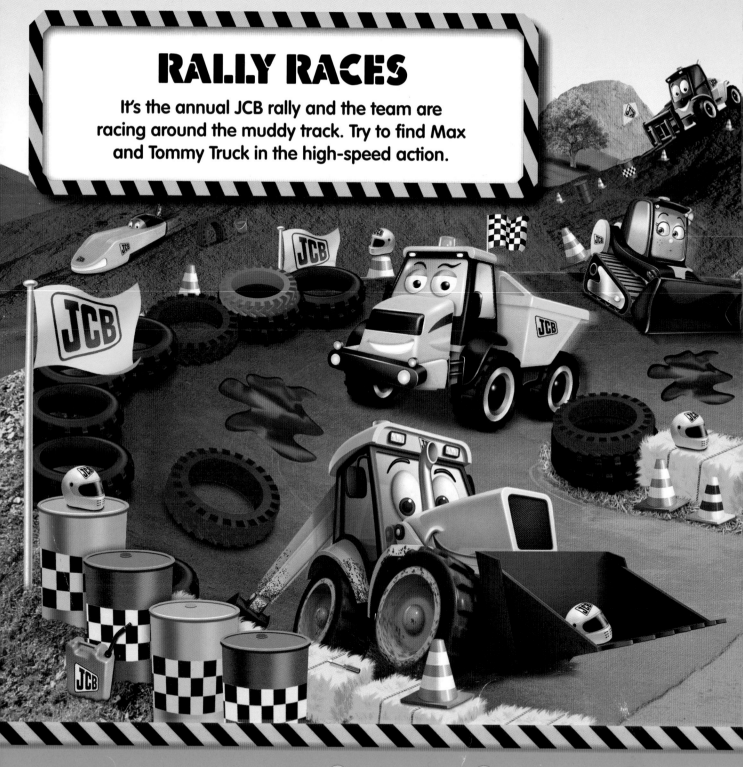

RALLY RACES

It's the annual JCB rally and the team are racing around the muddy track. Try to find Max and Tommy Truck in the high-speed action.

Great! Can you find these items too?

1 JCB trophy

3 checkered flags

4 mud puddles

What a race! Who do you think is going to win?

6 JCB flags

8 racing helmets

10 red tires

BUILD IT UP

Joey and his JCB friends are busy on a high-rise building site. Can you spot Elvis Excavator and Roxy Robot working hard somewhere up high?

Now can you find all
these items too?

1 red oil drum

3 blue crates

4 jackhammers

7 cement bags

8 warning signs

10 hard hats

FARMYARD FUN

The JCB team are helping out on Mr. Bamford's farm.
Search the scene and try to find Doug Dumptruck
and Tommy Truck working hard.

 Well done!
Can you find
all of these
things too?

1 combine harvester

3 piles of hay

4 chickens

6 blue wheelbarrows

8 pitchforks

10 bags of feed

What a noisy place! Who is loading feed into the barn?

QUARRY CHAOS

It's a busy day at the quarry, as the JCB friends move and sort all the different materials. Can you spot Marty Mixer and Larry Loadall on the messy site?

Can you spot these things too?

1 diamond

3 blue pipes

4 piles of debris

6 cones

8 pickaxes

15 yellow bricks

REST AND REPAIR

The JCB team have come back to JCB HQ to relax and get cleaned up. Where are Dan Dozer and Larry Loadall relaxing?

 Now try to find these items too.

 1 hose

2 red gas cans

4 buckets of water

6 wrenches

8 JCB banners

15 spare wheels

Not everyone gets to rest. Which JCB friends are missing?

BRIDGE BUILDERS

Team JCB are hard at work building a new bridge.
Can you spot Joey JCB and Freddie Fastrac
on the busy construction site?

Can you spot these things too?

1 gas pump

3 storage containers

4 green crates

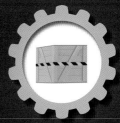

7 arrow signs

8 orange lights

10 safety jackets

READY FOR TAKE-OFF

The JCB team are at an airport to repair the runway.
Hidden among the planes and luggage are
Dan Dozer and Rex Roller. Can you find them?

Great!
Now try to
find these
items too.

1 yellow hot-air balloon   2 luggage trolleys   4 red barriers

 **6 moving stairs**

8 wind socks

 **15 blue suitcases**

Up, up, and away! Who is loading a special engine onto Tommy Truck?

IN THE FOREST

The JCB friends are busy replanting and restoring the forest. Hidden among the trees somewhere are Joey JCB and Doug Dumptruck. Can you find them?

1 tree shredder

3 cabins

4 piles of sawdust

7 bags of seeds

8 red leaves

10 trees

FUN AT THE FAIR

What a hard day's work! Now it's time to relax and have some fun. Can you spot all 11 JCB friends having fun at the JCB theme park?

Excellent! Now try to find all these things too.

1 JCB slide

2 cameras

4 signposts

6 tickets

8 bags of popcorn

15 JCB balloons

Roll up! Roll up! Which three friends are enjoying the slide?

WELL DONE!

You've found everything, but how closely were you paying attention?
Can you find these ten things in each JCB scene too?

1 blue JCB hot-air balloon

1 green wheelbarrow

1 purple oil drum

1 JCB gas can

1 orange safety jacket

1 blue tire

1 red bucket

1 JCB cone

1 JCB kite

1 screwdriver

BONUS!

A shadow of Joey JCB is stamped on one scene. Go back and see if you can spot it!